MW00994679

The Paris Apartment

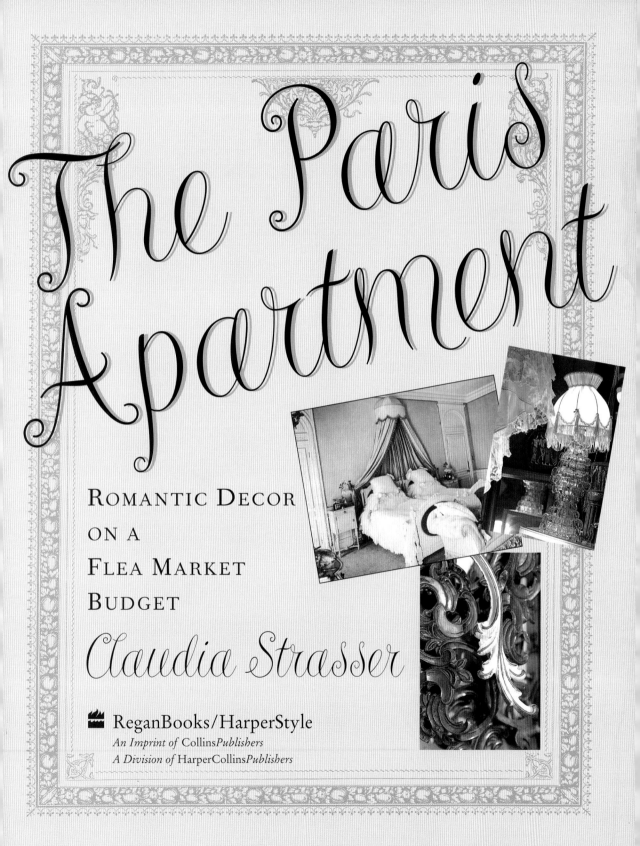

The Paris Apartment

ROMANTIC DECOR
ON A
FLEA MARKET
BUDGET

Claudia Strasser

ReganBooks/HarperStyle
An Imprint of Collins Publishers
A Division of HarperCollins Publishers

Photography credits:

Tim White/Outline:	page x
Jim Estrin/New York Times:	page xv
Mark Seliger/Outline:	page 124
Jen Fong:	page 144
John Muggenborg:	page iii, metal decoration; page 4, figurine; page 5, door knob parts; page 29, before photo; page 53, before photo; page 94, before photo; page 107, before photo

All other photographs were taken by Irene Sperber.

THE PARIS APARTMENT. Copyright © 1997 by Claudia Strasser. All rights reserved. Printed in the United States No part of this book may be used or reproduced in any manner whatsoever without written permission except in the case of brief quotations embodied in critical articles and reviews. For information address Collins Publishers, 10 East 53rd Street, New York, NY 10022.

HarperCollins books may be purchased for educational, business, or sales promotional use. For information please write: Special Markets Department, HarperCollins Publishers, Inc., 10 East 53rd Street, New York, NY 10022.

FIRST EDITION

Designed by Joel Avirom, Jason Snyder, and Meghan Day Healey

Library of Congress Cataloging-in-Publication Data
Strasser, Claudia, 1965–
The Paris apartment / by Claudia Strasser.
     p.   cm.
ISBN 0-06-039169-3
1. House furnishings. 2. Interior decoration. I. Title.
TX311.S83   1997
747'.88314—dc20   96-25669

97 98 99 00 01 /   10 9 8 7 6 5 4 3 2

To you

Beauty is everlasting and dust is for a time.
—Marianne Moore

CONTENTS

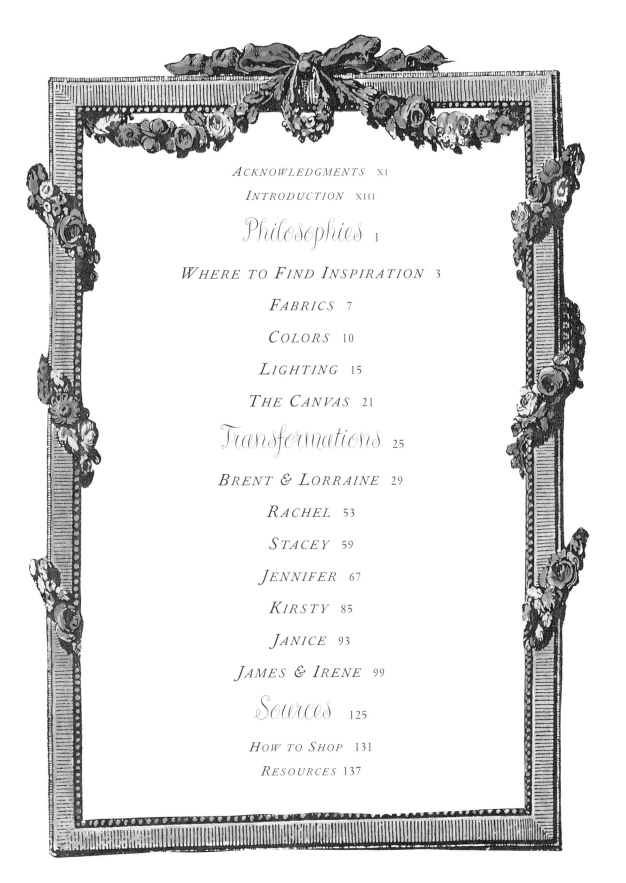

*I*t's almost impossible to express more thanks to Leigh Sperber, friend, producer, troubleshooter, coauthor, liaison, and overall savior. And, as she will never let me forget, were it not for her total devotion, this project would still be just a great concept.

May all who read this have such a dedicated sister.

And of course, to all who worked nonstop to meet deadlines and make it happen . . . Dad and Colin, Urs, Jack, Jim, Lori, David, Irene, Debbie, Rachel, Rachel, and Rachel, Connie Janusz and Kaori, Jen, Stacey, Kirsty, Brent, Lorraine, James, Billy, Irene, Janice, Kelly, Amy, Frank, Mum, Evan, John Muggenborg, Nadine, Denny, everyone at Archangel Antiques, Candlelande, Kristin, Todd, and Jennifer at ReganBooks, Meghan and Joel, and a special thanks to Judith Regan and her limitless imagination.

ACKNOWLEDGMENTS

I first fell in love with Paris when I went to work there as an au pair. The entire city had a feeling of luxury about it, especially the fabulous old apartments. These were the apartments I'd always dreamed of, yet I found they inspired new fantasies, too. I longed to lounge on a chaise in a Paris apartment, wrapped in a silk robe, writing letters on creamy stationery.

When I returned to the States, I wanted to live the fantasy. I imagined abandoning the au pair for the princess and sleeping not in a bedroom but in a boudoir. I had to undergo this metamorphosis on a shoestring budget, but Ikea and hand-me-downs would never do. Scouring flea markets, rummage sales, and even the Salvation Army, I found trinkets and furnishings that evoked an ambience of Parisian indulgence. From these I created an apartment that recalls a bygone era when daily life was slower,

INTRODUCTION

If one is lucky,
a solitary fantasy can
totally transform
one million realities.

—MAYA ANGELOU

more luxurious, more romantic. My boudoir is now a seductive refuge from the realities of city living.

To some, my apartment may seem more like a genie's bottle than a practical place to live. But the Paris Apartment aesthetic is about meeting *all* your needs. Your apartment is like a friend or lover: It's there to help you relax, to cheer you up, to make you feel comfortable and secure and desirable. Why come home to an apartment as cold and sterile as the office you just left? When opulence is so affordable, why not surround yourself with rich colors, sumptuous fabrics, and vintage furniture?

When real life intrudes on your fantasy apartment in the form of radiators, televisions, window gates, and microwaves, a little ingenuity can preserve a mood of sensuality. Even a tiny apartment can become a jewelry box of personal trea-

sures, for creativity thrives on a challenge. Any apartment can be transformed into an extension and expression of who you really are. Tap your fantasies and let them guide you as you redecorate. If you let yourself live among the beautiful things you've always pined for, you will feel like the goddess, movie star, or princess who lives deep inside you. Making dreams come true is what the Paris Apartment is really all about.

Philosophia

In all things in nature
there is something marvelous.

—ARISTOTLE

*I*f you take the time to really look at the world, you'll discover visual excitement all around you. You can find beauty wherever you go—on the street and in shops, at movies and museums, while traveling and visiting friends, or in the pages of catalogs and books. We miss so much of life's pleasure when, in our headlong rush through each day, we forget to pay attention to our surroundings. Yet the simple act of observation—looking up to contemplate the architecture of nearby buildings, or lingering to absorb their details—can illuminate your inner world. That's where inspiration starts.

The inspirations behind the Paris Apartment aesthetic date back centuries. Period styles such as seventeenth-century baroque, eighteenth-century rococo, nineteenth-century neoclassical or twentieth-

Where to Find Inspiration

The softest things in the world overcome the hardest things in the world.

—LAO-TZU

century art deco recall long-lost ways of living. Hundreds of years ago, Parisians started painting their walls in rich, vibrant hues and decorating their ceilings with murals. They made abundant use of draperies, curtains, swags, and valances so that not only their windows but their doorways, beds, and walls nestled in voluptuous silks and velvets. They brought fresh flowers and potted plants indoors, transporting the vitality of nature to their rooms. And they filled their homes with knick-knacks and details like prints and paintings, candelabra and clocks, porcelain figurines and cut-glass candy dishes.

You can sense this history in the things you see every day. The shapes all around you—in ornamental ironwork or stonework, in cornices, finials, and filigrees—can take your imagination back through time. Even in quirky old door handles, hinges, switch plates, light fixtures, and chair legs you can discover what Cleopatra, Lorenzo de' Medici,

Louis XIV, and Coco Chanel knew about luxury: It's all in the details. The handcrafted beauty of a carved antique chair leg, the superior workmanship of a vintage end table, remind you that you deserve the very best; unique objects like these pamper you. To own a lamp shade or an armoire with a past is to inherit its history. Its age, its style, and the materials it's made of usher you into another, more elegant moment in time.

As you let inspiration flow, follow your intuition to the colors, fabrics, and themes that appeal to you. Let your essential self—the fanciful, erotic, or outrageous personality you may hide from others—make your decorating decisions. Perhaps, inexplicably, you'll be drawn to certain pieces or textures or realms that somehow speak to you. Maybe you've always had a passion for your great-aunt's cloisonné collection or for the Victorian settee your best friend inherited. One piece can spark an entire idea, instantly crystallizing the possibilities. Listen to your impulses, and before long you'll know exactly what kind of apartment will satisfy your needs and cravings. This will make the entire redecorating process—the planning, the shopping, and the work—easy and fun.

Finding Your Fantasy

Every Paris Apartment starts with a fantasy. If you're not sure what yours might be, just remember that the operative word is "luxury." Envision your ideal setting, focusing on the details that make you feel pampered. Does a unified stylistic theme emerge? Do you mix and match a variety of looks? Either approach will work, as long as you base all your decorating decisions on the same original theme. Here are a few fantasy ideas to jog your imagination:

- Cleopatra's Egypt
- Ancient Greece
- Roman baths
- Mandarin China
- Moorish palaces
- Mayan temples
- Polynesian islands
- Medieval towers
- Elizabethan London
- Gothic cathedrals
- Venetian piazzas
- Arabian harem tents
- Cinderella's castle
- Mediterranean villas
- The Taj Mahal
- Baroque ballrooms
- Rococo châteaus

- Versailles
- Neoclassical manors
- Victorian parlors
- Viennese coffeehouses
- Art nouveau town houses
- Ocean liners
- Edwardian sitting rooms
- Art deco penthouses
- Parisian cabarets
- Hollywood dressing rooms
- Prewar Berlin
- 1940s Manhattan
- Las Vegas honeymoon suites
- The Plaza Hotel

Fabrics

What is the throne?—a bit of wood gilded and covered with velvet.

—NAPOLEON BONAPARTE

Have you ever noticed how gorgeous you feel when you wear that velvet cocktail dress, silk scarf, or satin negligee? Nothing thrills the senses quite like fine fabric, whether it's fresh, linen sheets, a toasty cashmere topcoat, or an ancient, buttery-soft T-shirt. The same goes for the fabrics you use to decorate a room: They wrap you in sensations of extravagance and comfort, arousing, yet soothing, the body. As the clothing of a room, fabric is the foundation of the Paris Apartment philosophy.

We "hit the sack" in cozy bedding, frame our view of the world with flowing draperies, adorn our furniture with pretty upholstery, and veil decorating trouble spots with skirts and curtains. Spare to ostentatious, fabric sets the mood of a room. Smooth, fluid silks and satins can summon sensations of coolness; lush, heavy velvets can generate real warmth. The more fabric you use, the stronger the statement and the more sumptuous the effect. When you go beyond cloth to include feather boas, leathers, rugs and carpets, sheepskins and fake or natural fur, the possibilities expand even more.

Don't be afraid to indulge your every fabric fantasy. Shop with your eyes closed and touch everything . . . if it feels good, buy it! Take your booty home and surround yourself with layer after billowing layer. Drape it over everything, let it spill onto the floor. Dressed in an abundance of fabric, any room will entice the senses and gratify your appetite for grandeur.

Choosing and Using Fabrics

For the most luxurious results, buy the best fabric you can afford. Don't skimp on velvets, and buy 100 percent cottons or mostly cotton blends. Fabrics and fibers that can help fulfill your Paris Apartment fantasy include:

- silk
- satin
- velvet
- brocade
- lace

- tapestry
- cheesecloth
- mohair
- cotton
- rayon

Stripes and animal prints have an exotic, antique air, as do faux and antique furs and sheepskins. Whatever your choice, look for vintage fabric to save money and bring the past into your space. A few tatters add character, and many of yesterday's fabric designs cannot be found today. Old curtains can be converted into upholstery or altered to fit your windows.

The two main uses for fabric in any Paris Apartment are upholstery and curtains. Chairs and sofas should be covered with strong and durable, yet sensuous, fabrics such as velvet and mohair. Boudoir and slipper chairs—or any small chair that only you use—look good in satin. In the bathroom, terry cloth in many shades makes a cute covering for small chairs and stools. Fake fur is well suited to stools, benches, lounge chairs, and sofas, while zebra and leopard prints add a playful touch to dining-room and boudoir chairs.

Almost any fabric can work as drapery, especially satin, velvet, silk, and mohair. Inexpensive cheesecloth makes excellent sheer under curtains, preserving privacy while letting in light. Vintage curtains not only offer the advantage of being pre-sewn, complete with linings and gathers, they often come with matching valances and tiebacks. Whichever fabric you choose, your drapery will draw attention to your windows and accentuate ceiling height. Keep them large to puddle on the floor.

Sometimes it seems that our emotions are ruled by color: We feel blue, see red, turn green with envy, have black moods, and get tickled pink. Clearly, color is central to your apartment's rebirth, because the shades you choose both express who you are and affect how you feel. As a retreat from the gray, monotonous, postindustrial world, your home should embrace you with vibrant colors that renew your spirits and your energy. Like makeup, which can instantly turn you from wholesome mother to refined professional to smoldering vixen, color can completely alter the mood of a room, transforming an ordinary space into a miniature paradise—or den of iniquity.

Don't be afraid to fill your private sanctuary with lots of color. Banish barren white walls and lifeless beige carpeting from your home forever; immerse yourself in the

Colors

Perfumes, colors and sounds echo one another.

—Charles Baudelaire

robust, vivacious hues your soul craves. In eighteenth-century Paris they mixed colors in bold combinations: yellow with violet, pink with gold, azure with lime, emerald with crimson. This Parisian palette reflects a belief that beauty is a necessity, that a room doesn't work if it fails to give pleasure. Indulge yourself in color, and the workaday world will soon seem far away.

Color Combinations

You can use as many or as few colors as you like to transform your space. A single favorite color can serve as the foundation and backdrop for all the other elements in a room, or a riot of many colors can allow complete freedom when you accessorize. One classic approach is to combine two colors of your choice with white and silver or with white and gold. Silver gives a more feminine feeling to a room, while gold is essentially more masculine. A typically feminine room, for instance, might use silver, white, celadon, and blue on rinceau-treated walls, topped by a yellow ceiling and furnished with silver and gray satins. A more masculine space might have pumpkin walls, gold trim, and a navy ceiling and be accessorized with navy, burgundy, and gold satins.

Colors and combinations found in nature—the colors of living things—are the most pleasing and perfect. These include pale, bright, and dark greens, reds, yellows, pinks, blues, oranges, and purples. As a rule of thumb, use three main colors in each room to integrate its various elements. Dark colors will make a room feel snug and warm, but remember that they may also make a room seem smaller. Lighter colors can be cooler and more airy and will make a room seem larger. Your color choice depends on what kind of atmosphere you want to create. Two tips when choosing paint:

Colors always look darker on those sample strips in the store than they will in your apartment; always use water-based latex, which is far easier to work with and to clean up. Other than that, go wild!

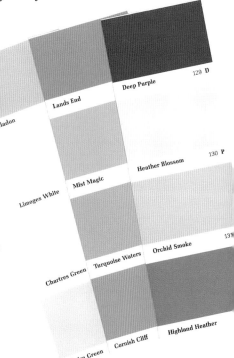

Celadon
Lands End
Deep Purple   129 D
Limoges White   Mist Magic
Heather Blossom   130 P
Chartres Green   Turquoise Waters   Orchid Smoke   131
Loire Green   Cornish Cliff   Highland Heather

Water- or Oil-Based?

Whenever you can—and you almost always can—use latex paint when you redecorate. The inexpensive water-based stuff dries quickly and cleans up easily with soap and water, even coming off floors, rugs, and clothing without a trace. Water-based polyurethane is readily available and has made a lot of formerly difficult finishing jobs a whole lot easier. Durable latex even works great on furniture, opening up a world of restoration possibilities. For furniture as well as walls, you can use water as a medium, or thinner, to create transparent washes of different colors, which you can layer over each other to add dimension to flat surfaces. Once dry, the high-gloss, semigloss, and eggshell finishes are easily kept clean with soap and water, while flat paint around light switches and doorknobs can take quick touch-ups with a small brush.

Costly oil-based paint, by contrast, takes forever to dry, smells awful, and is hard to clean up. Unfortunately, silver and gold paint is generally oil-based; to make cleaning a little easier, choose the less noxious orange-peel variety of turpentine. On the plus side, spray paint makes refinishing metal furniture a breeze—just make sure to remove all rust and dirt first.

DON'T PAINT BY THE NUMBERS

Always remember and never forget that the colors you see on paint swatches in the store will look brighter and more vibrant on your walls. To get the effect you really want, buy the tint one or two shades deeper than you intended.

Lighting

Light seeking light doth light of light beguile.

—William Shakespeare

Shimmering with glamour and excitement, Paris, the City of Light, sparkles all night, every night, like a diamond necklace. As bewitching by night as by day, the city loves to show off its evening wear. Likewise, your apartment—where you may spend more evenings than daytime hours—will look its best when its lighting glows like a rare gem. You already know that no matter how spectacular your clothing and makeup, a good piece of jewelry can make you even more stunning, while a mismatched or tacky piece can totally ruin the effect. The same holds true for a room. The right lighting will enhance its advantages; the wrong lighting will emphasize its faults.

Lighting is a necessity in your apartment, but it can also be fun. Dimmers and

three-way or colored lightbulbs can change the mood at the flick of a switch. Vintage lamps, lamp shades, fixtures, and especially chandeliers can become decorative focal points that hold the entire room together. The lighting you choose will be just as important as furniture, fabrics, and colors in creating an enchanting space. Depending on your desires, your lighting scheme can emanate romance, mystery, gaiety, or grace.

Harsh, bright lights, bare bulbs, fluorescents, and most overhead lighting are strictly forbidden in your haven of restful civility. Instead, use soft, indirect illumination that will make you look and feel your best. Sconces, mirrors, and a profusion of candles give off the seductive light that life is meant to be lived by. And, of course, make the most of natural light sources, such as windows and skylights. Like a beacon in the night or a light at the end of a tunnel, a well-lit apartment will guide you home to safety and embrace you in comfort.

Lights!

Because lighting pulls the room together, I keep my approach simple:

- For overhead lighting, use a chandelier; it should hang in the center of the room.

- Standing chandeliers, especially when placed by the bed, are fun and dramatic.

- The bare bulbs of a chandelier can be covered with tiny shades dyed to complement the room's color scheme. Shades trimmed with fringe, satin, velvet, or animal prints really bring a chandelier to life. Hang extra crystals, rhinestones, or other baubles from the chandelier to make it even more extravagant.

- Bedside lamps make a boudoir warm and seductive.

- A standing lamp placed by an armchair makes for a cozy and inviting reading spot.

- Lamp shades determine the overall effect of a lamp—changing the shade transforms the lamp. A ruffled shade creates one look, while a tailored plaid shade on the same lamp creates an entirely different effect.

- Acquire the lamp shade of your dreams from a custom lamp-shade maker, who will cover the skeleton of your choice with any fabric you desire. Think of the possibilities!

- The best natural light is morning sunshine filtered through sheer curtains, onto the bed where you're enjoying breakfast on a tray. If really good natural light is not available, stick to fabulous artificial light.

*O*nce history, fabric, color, and light have inspired your heart's desire, take a good, long look at your apartment. How can you paint your vision on this blank canvas? How can you inscribe your fantasies on this tabula rasa? An empty room is full of possibilities, so it's important to clean house before you create a French boudoir, a Roman bath, or an Edwardian parlor.

Figure out which of your possessions you love and which simply take up space. Some pieces may fit into your plans perfectly and others may work once they've been repainted or repaired. There will, however, be plenty of things that simply must go: the cinder-block and lumber bookshelves, the flea-bitten recliner, the milk-crate nightstands. Anything hopeless, useless, or charmless should find a new life with a friend, as a charitable donation, or at the dump. To make the process of elimination easier, start with small objects and work your

The Canvas

For his art did express
a quintessence even from
nothingness.

—JOHN DONNE

way up to larger ones, perhaps sorting everything into "yes," "no," and "maybe" piles. Consider each item carefully, evaluating its potential and tossing anything that doesn't make the grade.

Now step back and see what's left. Imagine ways to turn your space into a stage set for a sumptuous lifestyle. You will probably need to add some special furnishings—make a list at home before you head for the flea market. As you begin the metamorphosis, notice hidden treasures that emerge when you strip off paint, pull up linoleum, or move the couch. Your idea will evolve as you bring new pieces into the room or change the color of your walls. Go with the flow and let your fantasy emerge on its own. A room that comes from the heart will feed your soul . . . just follow your dreams to the Paris Apartment!

Where to Begin

—

$\mathcal{A}$ny space can fulfill your fantasy, so don't feel confined by your home's layout or architecture. The shapes of your windows and doorways, the existing floor coverings, or other features may inspire you or suggest a theme, but if they don't match your mood, don't despair. You can completely transform any space with colors, drapery, mirrors, murals, and other tools, even turning a cramped, windowless box into a breezy garden or an undersea grotto. Once you've chosen a theme, select a palette to match. Evaluate potential wall and window treatments, making a list for your trips to the hardware and fabric stores. Then evaluate your furnishings and determine what you need to buy, either as additions or replacements. Now it's off to the flea market, where further inspiration awaits!

Transformations

You are never given a wish
without also being given
the power to make it true.

—RICHARD BACH

*H*ave you ever heard yourself say, "This place would be great if only . . . "? As apartment dwellers, we usually pay too much for too little space with too many trouble spots. We move in with visions of home improvement dancing in our heads, but somehow our good intentions fade away after we decide where to put the television. Even if we had the time to fix up the place, the argument goes, we wouldn't have a clue as to what to do, and we definitely couldn't afford to do it. Actually, even the busiest, clumsiest, and brokest among us has everything it takes to create a fantasy apartment. Start with one room and a little ingenuity, and *voilà!,* you're on your way.

The rooms made over in the pages of this book come from seven separate apartments, each occupied by real people with real needs and personalities. We could see some of their qualities and preferences in the things they already owned. Each room or apartment suggested additional possibilities, either right off the bat or after we started working.

With almost no time or money at our disposal, no special tools, and almost no skilled help, we realized many fantasies and even came up with some new ones. We mixed and matched, repainted and revamped, and pulled a few simple tricks out of our hat to completely reinvent these bedrooms, living rooms, dressing rooms, and baths. Before we started, we weren't sure we could pull it off, but we're here to tell you: If we can do it, anyone can!

The Bottom Line

If you embrace the Paris Apartment philosophies, you can live in luxury without spending a lot of money. A few special pieces, some fabric, and plenty of color can evoke the opulence of any far-off place or time. The apartments shown in these pages required an average investment of only $1,800, compared with double, triple, or many times that amount for a standard redecoration. You can expect to spend the following on a full-fledged, no-holds-barred Paris Apartment transformation:

Paint	*$70*
Minor repairs	*20*
Hardware	*20*
Trimmings	*60*
Fabric	*200*
Rugs	*200*
Furniture	*1,000*
Lighting	*200*
Objets d'art	*30*
TOTAL	*$1,800*

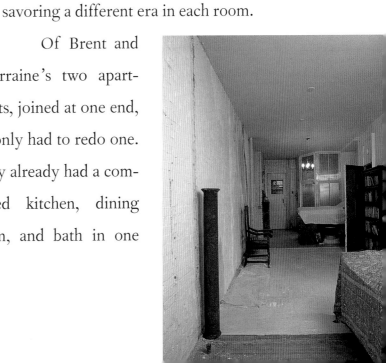

Brent and Lorraine live in two long, narrow, Alphabet City apartments that immediately reminded us of train cars. Standing in the raw space, we conjured up images of rail travel the way it used to be: steamer trunks, dining cars set with crystal and silver, brandy in the salon car, porters in crisp uniforms. The passengers on this train would be a New York psychotherapist and makeup artist, and they would travel not through space but through layers of consciousness, far away from their rough and sometimes scary neighborhood. Behind closed doors they could go back in time, savoring a different era in each room.

Brent & Lorraine

A private railroad car is not an acquired taste. One takes to it at once.

—ELEANOR ROBSON BELMONT

Of Brent and Lorraine's two apartments, joined at one end, we only had to redo one. They already had a completed kitchen, dining room, and bath in one unit, so they needed to add a living room, bedroom, and dressing area in the other. We started from scratch because the space was totally open and unfinished. A plywood half wall separated the living area from Brent's gold-leafing workshop at one end, the front door gave onto the apartment's midsection, and a rear door opened onto a courtyard at the other end.

We first moved the wall back to open up the living quarters, a task that required only a few basic power tools and some muscle. To create the rooms they needed, we mentally divided the empty living space into compartments, just like on a train. Closest to the workshop would be the dressing room, while the bedroom would occupy the quieter end of the apartment and the living room would fill the area in between. Each compartment would have its own palette and historical theme.

Dressing Room
Brent's art deco armoire and the wooden workshop wall inspired us to build on the railroad theme and create a handsome dressing room reminiscent of the Orient Express. Dark wood paneling, rich fabrics, and royal colors could evoke the pampered air we were going for. We sanded and varnished the dark wood floor, painted the walls crimson, and finished the ceiling in

gold. To divide the dressing area from the living room, we tacked up a forest green velvet curtain that ensures privacy and lends a theatrical flavor to both spaces. Cheesecloth hung above the plywood half wall lets natural light filter in from the workroom.

Brent and Lorraine already owned most of the furniture that we used for this room. A quick sanding and a coat of stain rejuvenated Brent's armoire. On top, we

arrayed some of his old books and bookends, as well as a collection of vintage shaving-tonic bottles. At the flea market we found just the right vanity and matching stool for Lorraine, which we adorned with picture frames, perfume bottles, and an antique vase to hold her makeup brushes. The his-and-hers arrangement gives Brent and Lorraine the ideal setting to display the many knickknacks they've collected over the years.

To light the space, we brought in a pair of lamps from the 1920s; a silk-shaded, hand-painted porcelain lamp from the 1930s; and a 1940s lamp with a striped, scalloped shade. A bit tattered, perhaps, but still beautiful. For an extra touch, we finished up with some fresh flowers.

Wall Wizardry

If you are lucky enough to have a brick wall, you can approach it in a number of ways to reflect your personality. You can leave it as is, repaint it, chip off old paint, or completely plaster it over. For plaster walls, small holes can be patched with some spackle and a putty knife, while large holes can be taken care of with plaster of paris mixed in a large bucket.

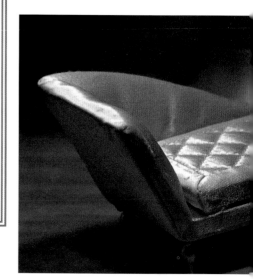

Bedroom   The idea for the bedroom started with a crumbling plaster wall that didn't exactly look promising. As we chipped at it to prepare it for a coat of plaster, we began to like what emerged. Under the surface, we found layer upon layer of old paint that produced an interesting effect when exposed by our work. We chipped the entire wall and left it looking like part of a ruined medieval castle. No need to look any farther for inspiration!

Succumbing to the gothic mood, we painted the bedroom's other walls a dark midnight blue. The wooden floor turned to stone under the paintbrushes of Janusz and Kaori, professional muralist friends of ours, as they laid down a layer of faux slate. Over their shadowy mural, we applied three protective coats of latex polyurethane. In keeping with our archaic theme, we decided that the windows should be stained glass. Brent and Lorraine happen to have a friend who makes

stained glass, and she agreed to do two panels. We could have imitated the effect with stained-glass paint or bought and hung an old piece of stained glass from an architectural salvage store. Instead, we used the stained-glass theme to link the bedroom with the dressing room at the opposite end of the apartment,

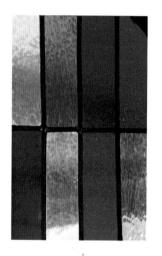

painting the door on the plywood wall with stained-glass colors.

To separate the bedroom from the living room, we made a curtain of sheer, iridescent blue-green-gold fabric that has a sword and sorcery feel to it. As in the dressing room, we preserved natural light and added privacy with cheesecloth drapery. We hung it on the window that has no stained glass and used it to veil the backdoor. A valance-style canopy on the wall at the head of the bed recalls regal tents and castles; made of nineteenth-century French linen, it came from a small shop Lorraine loves. While shopping at another store, she fell head over heels for a fake chinchilla throw, but it was ridiculously overpriced. We found the same fabric at a wholesaler and bought twice as much for an eighth of the price, so Lorraine got her throw anyway.

The faux throw went onto the bed for a decidedly imperial

Layer upon Layer

Artists know that different shades of paint layered over each other can create the illusion of three dimensions on a two-dimensional surface. But you don't have to be an artist to take advantage of this effect. For instance, you can add a faux stone wall or floor to your home with nothing more than white, gray, and black paint. Over a coat of basic gray, apply irregular smudges and patches of lighter and darker shades to evoke the bulges and hollows of rough-hewn stone blocks. When dry, paint in the thin black outlines of the "rocks."

effect. Perched high off the floor atop two dressers, the bed is no triumph of design, but its uncommon height had a fairy-tale quality that spoke of princesses and peas. Rather than replacing it, we masked the supporting dressers with an extra-long, blue velvet dust ruffle that fit in perfectly with the medieval theme. We also made use of their existing nightstand, lamp, and empire table to fill out the room's furnishings.

Drawbridges and jousting matches came to mind when we stumbled on an eccentric iron candelabra at Candlelande in the East Village; it went under the canopy, at the head of the bed. Brent and Lorraine also found a gothic chandelier that we had rewired. We hung it from the ceiling, below a foam-core medallion we added. Throughout the room, we found perches for lots of candles, which radiate traces of torchlight when lit. When we were finished, Brent and Lorraine had a bedchamber that would make any monarch proud.

Live with the gods.
—MARCUS AURELIUS

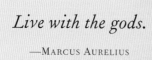

Living Room

Framed by a velvet curtain at one end and billows of iridescence at the other, the living room seemed to offer a thousand decorating possibilities. It also posed some serious challenges, the kind that inspire miraculous solutions. First of all, the space had no windows. To make up for the lack of natural light, we decided on a pale, airy palette that would also set this room off from the others.

The lumpy old walls smoothed out under a coat of plaster, which, after it dried, we painted a light celery green. Color alone immediately turned the room into an ancient Roman grotto, an effect that was intensified when we brought in some clay pots that Brent and Lorraine already owned. We stepped farther back in

time by toning down the walls with tinted washes. These consisted of one part off-white latex, three parts water, and a squirt of a pigment called Tints-All. Using a sponge mop, we applied three washes: one raw umber, one burnt sienna, and one avocado. The irresistibly ancient atmosphere then prompted us to paint faux swags along the tops of the walls.

Situated firmly in antiquity, we found ourselves in a Pompeiian courtyard that just had to have a goldfish pond at its

Tints and Washes

—

For dramatic effect, turn your wall or furniture into an instant antique with washes in several colors. These translucent tints are layered one over another to give the illusion of age and depth. For instance, a tan or green wall coated with a darkened yellow wash give the impression of nicotine staining. Whatever your color choices, you will see your wall or dresser acquire an entirely different—and entirely impressive—character as the coats go on.

Walls

1. Paint the surface with a solid coat of a basic, light color such as off-white, misty green, or pale yellow.

2. Choose three or four complementary shades of the pigment called Tints-All, such as umber, sienna, gold, or avocado. Also buy some white or off-white latex flat or eggshell with which to mix it.

3. Mix the first wash in a paint tray, making enough for the entire coat so the color is uniform. One part latex, three parts water, and a squeeze or two of Tints-All produces a lovely wash. If it looks too dark, just thin it out with extra water.

4. Apply the wash with a natural sponge or a sponge mop or a rag, watching for drips. Wipe any drips immediately with a rag. Use extra wash in the corners and around details to produce a shading that simulates age. Blend adjoining areas with a rag, a dry paintbrush, or a natural sponge.

5. When the first wash is dry, repeat the process with two or three more washes of different colors. The layering effect produces an attractive texture and depth.

Furniture

1. Paint the surface with a solid coat of a basic, light color such as off-white, misty green, or pale yellow.

2. Add gold and silver highlights to carvings, edges, and other elevated contours.

3. Mix green or gold Tints-All with clear polyurethane and apply to the entire piece.

4. Add some dark brown Tints-All to the polyurethane and apply to joints, crevices, and other recessed contours. Blot with a sponge or paper towel to leave deeper areas darker and shallower areas lighter.

center. The wooden floor was hidden under a layer of yellowing off-white paint, so we called on our friend Janusz to give us a hand. We roughed up the surface with sand-paper, put Janusz to work, and before we knew it we were gazing into a trompe l'oeil pool of aquatic serenity. Using the same washes that had aged the walls, Janusz finished the surrounding floor to resemble courtyard pavement. We then protected his work with three coats of polyurethane.

Just a note: Trompe l'oeil is a tricky business, but not impossible to learn if you have the inclination. If not, there are plenty of starving artists in every city who hire out to paint all kinds of illusions on the cheap. Or we could have created a

similar effect simply by sanding and refinishing the floors and putting down a pale aquamarine area rug.

To enhance our vision of Pompeii, we had to overcome two more twentieth-century obstacles: some dangling old electrical wires and a cumbersome radiator and steam pipe opposite the front door.

Since these were the first things visitors saw when they stepped into the apartment, we had to disguise them expertly so they wouldn't ruin the mirage. After determining that the electrical wires carried no current, we simply snipped them off at the base. Then we considered the radiator.

Many home-improvement stores sell radiator covers, but we wanted something that would genuinely add to the room. The radiator, we decided, could become both a warm place to sit and a con-

sole table, while the steam pipe could serve as an additional visual division between the living room and the bedroom. We asked York, another friend, to help us out. We discussed the theme and he constructed a radiator cover of copper strips topped with a padded seat. Above this elegant perch we hung Brent's antique, gold-framed mirror and brought in some unusual candleholders.

For the living room as a whole, we found an art nouveau chandelier that, oddly enough, complemented the classical theme. We dyed its shades blue and added fringe, then hung it below a foam-core medallion we attached to the ceiling. Moving on to furniture, we made selections and placements that cost as little as possible while maximizing the room's sense of space, making sure to give the fishpond center stage. We added a poolside daybed for relaxing, with a hassock that can double as an end table. Across the room, a rococo table with two chairs offers an intimate dining grotto. A console table provides another spot to create pretty displays and toss keys. Finally, a few freestanding classical columns, a ficus and a palm tree, and plenty of flowers perfected the open-air, indoor courtyard.

Dyeing Fabrics

When you come upon a marvelous old lamp shade, throw rug, curtain, or other piece of vintage fabric—or a piece of upholstered furniture—don't pass it up just because it has a few stains or faded spots. Many fabrics can be renewed with dye, especially those in lighter colors and cotton or cotton blends (note: nylons won't always take dye; test a hidden patch beforehand). Even when dye doesn't completely camouflage imperfections, it will draw the eye away to admire the entire piece. Choose a color that complements your theme, and boil the water and mix your dye in the largest pot available. Immerse the entire item, if you can, or dunk it in portions. Alternately, you can paint the dye onto the fabric with a brush. For upholstered furniture, apply the dye generously but don't soak the stuffing. Even if the final results are not uniform, they will be charming.

Rachel desperately needed to make over the small bathroom in her apartment. It was the most basic of baths: white tile, white walls and ceiling, and generic fixtures. Visually barren to the point of institutional, it even lacked a window. The room offered none of the restful, rejuvenating qualities a bathroom is meant to have. Seeking ways to imbue the room with some of the true spirit of bathing, we looked to the art's ancient practitioners. The Greeks and Romans prized the soothing qualities of water and built grand public facilities where everyone could enjoy a good bath, sometimes for hours at a time. Thoughts of Greece and Rome gave way to visions of the brilliant blue Mediterranean Sea and the sparkling white houses of the Aegean islands. We decided to create a calming, revitalizing bathroom by evoking a holiday in the Greek isles.

Rachel

I have bathed in the Poem of the Sea . . .
devouring the green azures.

—Arthur Rimbaud

Bath First we chose a turquoise palette that reflects the blue hues of the Mediterranean. We painted the walls in easy-to-clean eggshell finish and left the ceiling in its original high-gloss white. (Never use matte paint in the bath—it too easily accumulates hard-to-remove stains and smudges.) Penciling in a decorative border along the top edge of the wall tile and the edge of the ceiling, our friend Julie painted an Aegean wave motif in black. We used an oil-based paint, but latex sealed with acrylic spray would do just as well. A few broken floor tiles needed replacing, a task easily accomplished with some matching tiles and waterproof epoxy.

Next came a striped canvas tent over the bathtub, fashioned to resemble a picturesque beach cabana. We laid a large piece of canvas on the living room floor and used masking tape to outline five-inch-wide stripes. Leaving alternate stripes unpainted, we filled in the black stripes with banner paint, a type of durable exterior paint. Along one edge we cut out a scalloped bottom, outlining the white scallops with a narrow black border. To hang the tent, we attached a one-inch-wide strip of self-stick Velcro to the top edge of the wall above the bathtub's long side, securing it with small nails at four-inch intervals. With a corresponding strip affixed to the tent's top edge, we joined the canvas to the wall. Draping the scalloped edge over the shower-curtain rod, we allowed the tent to dip gently from ceiling to rod. We folded the corner like a bed-sheet and tacked it in place with a needle and thread.

Taking the tent theme one step farther, we used soft white cotton fabric to fashion a sink skirt that would hide the plumbing and create some storage space. With self-stick Velcro, we improvised gathers along the sink's bottom edge, cutting a slit up the middle to give easy access to the under-sink area. A few stitches attached a bow of turquoise ribbon above the opening.

Wall Stencils

Painting a stenciled border onto a wall is a cheap and easy way to add pizzazz to any room. You can do the job with any kind of paint (latex is easiest), or for small jobs you can buy special tubes of stenciling paint. Premade stencils are available in many designs, but they can be expensive. If you want to save money, or if you can't find the pattern you want, you can make your own stencil:

1   *Look for ideas in art and architecture books on the eras that appeal to you.*

2   *Purchase an 8½ × 11-inch sheet of folder-weight oak tag and brush one side with linseed oil as a sealant.*

3   *Draw about a 6-inch segment of the design and cut it out with an X-Acto knife.*

4   *Hold the stencil flat against the wall with the linseed-coated side facing out. Carefully paint in the stencil with a brush or a sponge, working gently to keep the cut-out edges from fraying.*

5   *Align the edge of the stencil with the end of the painted pattern and continue.*

6   *When you've finished the stenciling, touch up the edges of the design with a small paintbrush for a hand-painted look.*

The starfish imagery summoned by a string of Rachel's star-shaped Christmas lights prompted us to turn the round mirror above the sink into a Hollywood-style one, using duct tape to arrange the lights around the edge. Attached with wire and duct tape, a costume-ball crown from a flea market became a sea-empress shade for the light fixture above. For the tub, we chose an inexplicably appropriate vintage 1940s shower curtain with a perfume-bottle pattern, tying it back with a satin sash. We then used a cascade of blue, green, and clear glass beads to decorate the lip and outside of the tub, gluing them on with water-proof epoxy.

The flea market provided all the room's furniture: A French découpage wastebasket went under the sink, and a decorative metal shelf—hung upside down—added charm as well as storage space at the foot of the tub. Another pretty metal shelf went up on the opposite wall as a handy place to store and hang extra linens. Below it, we placed a small vanity spray-painted silver. Antique hand towels, washcloths in a champagne bucket, and fresh green and blue soaps completed the room's seaside mood. Now Rachel can renew by the sea anytime just by drawing a hot bubble bath and lingering for a while.

The owner of a small antiques shop in Brooklyn, Stacey was like the mechanic whose car won't run: Her home was full of beautiful objects but it looked a mess. She wanted to make a change, starting with the bedroom. Her furniture and knickknacks have a distinctly Victorian feel that mirrors her formal, reserved persona. Underneath, though, she's sensuous and passionate. The contrast reminded us of how, just below the prim and proper public life of the Victorian age, there bubbled a seething sexuality. We began to think of the bordellos where that era whispered its secrets, and decided the bedroom was a perfect place to bring Stacey's inner self out of hiding.

Stacey

I generally avoid temptation unless I can't resist it.

—MAE WEST

Creating Drapes and Valances

—

*E*quipped with a curtain rod and some well-chosen fabric, it's easy to make luxuriant drapes and valances.

Curtains

1   Measure from the curtain rod to the sill or floor and add another foot or two to determine the length of fabric you need. The extra fabric will create wonderful billows and folds when the curtains are closed or tied back; with floor-length curtains, it will form sumptuous pools beneath your window.

2   Sew a strip of Velcro to the top, back edge of the fabric and sew its partner across the back, 4 inches lower. Drape the top of the fabric over the curtain rod and press the Velcro strips together. Voilà! You've just made a curtain!

Valances

A valance adds the finishing touch to drapery, enhancing the opulence of the flowing fabric. Fringe, tassels, and other trim can enrich the valance itself and make it one of your room's decorative highlights.

1   Measure the length of your curtain rod and add a foot or two to determine the length of fabric you need. The extra length gives you plenty of play to create gathers and dips. Allow a width of 6 to 10 inches, longer on the outside edges.

2   Leave the bottom edge straight or cut it into a scalloped, notched, or other pattern. Fold the edge back ¼ inch and tack to make a finished hem. Add fringe or other trimming if desired.

3   Hang the valance at the top of the curtain either by sewing it or with Velcro. Now admire your incredible handiwork!

Bedroom Stacey preferred not to paint, so we relied on fabric alone to dress up the room. We took the blue toile down from her windows and used it—along with a staple gun and some upholstery tacks—to cover some chairs and drape the upper half of her closet. Some of her red toile veiled the lower half of the closet. At the flea market, we found two valances that we easily adjusted with pins to fit above her windows. For curtains, we chose a brocade striped in burgundy and gold, buying twice as much as we needed. Doubling it up and slinging it over the curtain rods, we let the fabric overflow into puddles on the floor. We pinned the valances to the top and tied back the curtains with some antique flea market tassels. Finally, we layered Stacey's throw rugs to make the floor alluring to bedtime bare feet.

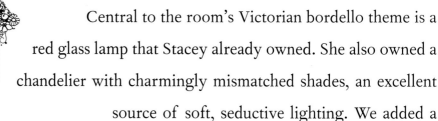

Central to the room's Victorian bordello theme is a red glass lamp that Stacey already owned. She also owned a chandelier with charmingly mismatched shades, an excellent source of soft, seductive lighting. We added a hand-painted porcelain table lamp with an oriental silk shade and set a sconce on the wall at the head of the bed. Finally finding a use for Stacey's box full of silk baby bonnets, we hung them around the sconce for shading.

As in every self-respecting bordello, the bed became a temple of pleasure. Sewing two cotton sheets together—one hunter green and one navy blue—we made a duvet cover with Velcro closures for Stacey's comforter. Her many pillows already boasted antique, hand-embroidered lace pillowcases; these just needed a trip to the Chinese laundry for cleaning, starching, and pressing. On top of it all, we tossed a faux-leopard throw that protects the linens and

Fabulous Duvet Covers

If you can't find just the right duvet cover for your comforter—or if the one you love costs too much—you can make one in a flash with two flat sheets. Favorite old sheets can become a comfy, pre-aged (and virtually free) duvet cover, while brand new 310-thread count sheets can lend the look and feel of luxury to your bed. Once you've chosen the sheets you like in the size required by your comforter, simply sew them together along three edges and secure Velcro, snaps, or buttons to the fourth side for closure. If you like, incorporate some winsome trim along the edges. Use old curtains or fabric pieces to make matching pillows in a variety of sizes and shapes—it's so easy and extremely economical.

makes Stacey's three sleek black cats feel right at home. The animal-print motif extends to a stool placed at the foot of the bed and flanked by two small urns.

Stacey loves old photographs and engravings, but did not know how best to display the large collection she had accumulated. We assembled a museum wall by hanging a profusion of pictures interspersed with some antique mirrors. Before this wall, we placed a small table for two, draped in a floor-length tablecloth and perfect for an amorous tête-à-tête. A flea market shelf cloaked in silk brought life to an empty corner of the room, giving Stacey a place to show off her most-prized collectibles. In another bare spot, we hung a mirror and created a Victorian washstand from a pitcher, a bowl and a tiny wooden table. The essential fresh flowers completed the room, setting the stage for her pursuit of happiness.

*J*ennifer, a working actress, lives in the famed Ansonia on the Upper West Side of Manhattan. Resembling a giant French château on the outside, the building is filled with glamorous apartments like Jen's studio. If only we all had high ceilings, inlaid wood floors, intricate moldings, curved walls, and mirrored French doors like these! The apartment suits Jen to a tee, maybe because she feels she was born in the wrong era. She has a passion for both the silent classics and technicolor films of Hollywood's golden age, so we decided to turn her studio into an elegant movie set where she can lounge about like Marlene Dietrich or Greta Garbo.

Jennifer

You can never be too good to yourself.

—Aɴᴏɴʏᴍᴏʊs

Dressing Room

Every movie star needs a dressing room, and Jen is no exception. Set off from the apartment's main living space, her circular entryway makes a perfect mini-salon where she can spoil herself, recharge her energy, and renew her spirits. After all, vanity is sanity!

We went with the room's existing palette of subdued colors that make a subtle backdrop for our star: pale mint for the walls, rich cream for the trim, and gold with black highlights. To conceal the adjoining kitchen, we hung a valance above the doorway and added two green panels to frame the sides.

Lighting for the dressing room consists of a metal floral chandelier that we found at a collectibles shop. It had essentially the same colors as the room, so we just touched it up a bit with latex craft paint. We hung it

below a foam-core medallion with rosettes painted to match the colors of the chandelier. Widely available at home-decorating stores, these medallions are lightweight and easy to handle, but they look like the real thing when painted. On the vanity, we placed one pair of standing flea market chandeliers; all we needed to do was add some shades.

The foyer had a built-in mirror under which Jen wanted to place a vanity. Rather than buying a traditional vanity, we found a large console table and painted it in crackling white. Because of the table's height, Jen needed extra-high vanity seating; we found an ideal swivel stool at an auction. On top of the vanity, we added

a movie star's three-way makeup mirror lined with twenty lightbulbs. Talk about star treatment! A dresser tray holds Jen's jewelry and perfume, while a hatbox filled with cosmetics sits poised for makeup jobs at auditions and on the go.

We embellished the dressing room with a satin slipper chair, which we reupholstered by using antique curtains to save money. The only other piece we added was a tall lingerie chest to hold all her personals. The rest of our work consisted of pure decoration: A figurine of Josephine Baker—the sexy, unique, and daring embodiment of everything the Paris Apartment represents—dances amid Jen's childhood collection of dollhouse furniture, perfectly at home on her own tiny stage. We hung some of Jen's props and costumes on the wall around the vanity, giving the space the atmosphere of a real Hollywood dressing room. Costumes like these—especially the old bustier dresses—can inspire big ideas for redecorating entire apartments, but in Jen's case, they play a supporting role. Starring in her dressing-room decor is her most prized stage costume, worn by an antique mannequin. Now when Jen is at home and surrounded by beauty, the boundaries between fantasy and reality are erased.

Reupholstering

It's easy to reupholster the seats of small stools, benches, ottomans, and straight-backed chairs.

1 *Turn the piece upside down and locate the screws or nails that secure the seat. Unscrew or pry them out and remove the seat.*

2 *Treating the seat like a package to be gift-wrapped, cover it with your new fabric and fasten the cloth to the bottom of the seat with staples or upholstery tacks. If you want a softer, puffier seat, add layers of batting or good foam before wrapping it.*

3 *Add trim or fringe to the edges with upholstery tacks or a hot-glue gun. Replace the seat.*

JENNIE HARBOUR

Studio   Jen's living area doubles as bedroom and office, presenting us with a special decorating challenge. Because we loved it so much, we continued the airy palette of the dressing area, but in here, as a counterpoint, we added a brilliant turquoise ceiling. The room's single, eleven-foot window was treated with satin curtains and a valance that we had the amazing good luck to recieve from among someone's castoffs. Slightly worn in a timeless way, it fit exactly over the top of the window. Tacked to the back of the valance, ten alternating pink-and-cream satin panels from the 1940s became

the curtains. We scattered plump, furry sheep-skins on the floor to pamper Jen's tired feet after days of auditioning. A mound of satin pillows tempts her to luxuriate like a film goddess, alluringly disheveled in her dressing gown. Everything in the room had to be smooth and sexy to the touch.

We established a softly glittering atmosphere with a chandelier, hanging the piece below another foam reproduction of a vintage ceiling medallion. Some wires remained exposed when we finished our work, so we wrapped them in silk. One of Jen's bedside tables received a glass lamp from a collectibles shop. To glam it up, we added long fringe and a pink satin ribbon to the edge of its wide shade. We placed a tiny glass 1930s lamp on the other night table, topped by a silk shade with tiny satin rosettes and swags.

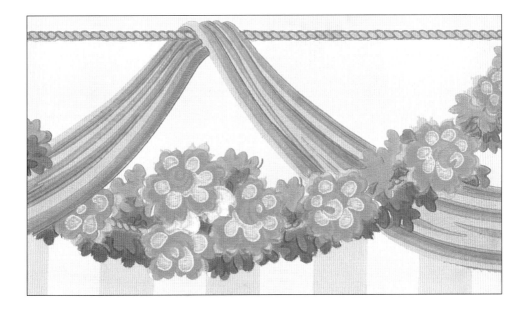

Dominating the center of the room, Jen's bed is a throne fit for any Hollywood queen. We located a distinctive French bedstead that echoes the apartment's châteaulike architecture, then hung the drapes behind it to suggest a theater stage. Then we stumbled upon the kind of fortuitous surprise that defines the Paris Apartment: When we began to clean her green night table with Windex, a layer of blue appeared. We decided to make the most of the situation and used the Windex to accent the drawer face and legs with a two-toned effect.

Nearby, an authentic overstuffed eighteenth-century Italian chair offers a comfy spot where Jen can completely relax and concentrate while reading scripts.

Keep It Clean

Upholstered furniture is always at risk from spills and day-to-day grime. Particularly in the dining room, choose dark shades of suede or mohair that can stand up to abuse and can mask accidents. To maintain the beauty of your chairs and sofas, use zippered slipcovers that can be removed for easy washing. Protect permanent upholstery with Scotchguard, and when it falls victim to a mishap, clean it with a little Woolite and cool water on a terry-cloth rag.

A three-piece, down-filled velvet settee lies in wait on the right side of the room. By its side stands a hand-painted Italian table and a French porcelain vase. Valances crown her bookshelves for a more polished look. We had planned to cover these with fresh fabric, but we found they took well to latex paint—much easier!

Jen also needed a serious work space where she can keep her computer, write, and work on ideas. We found her a kidney-shaped pastel-yellow desk and lit it with a standing chandelier. Next we needed to handle the more unromantic items such as the TV, VCR, stereo, and speakers. We perched her television and VCR atop a tall plaster pedestal. The stereo sits behind the desk for easy access and is hidden well. Since speakers should be celebrated, we enthroned them on tufted pink satin ottomans that we made from high, oval pieces of foam and adorned with long, silky fringe.

We personalized Jen's private backdrop with the knickknacks, books, and treasures she's collected over the years. An avid equestrian who lives with two dogs and three cats, Jen loves animals and cherishes her animal keepsakes. We created perches for them throughout the apartment, so she always has at least one in sight. The consummate blend of her professional and private personalities, Jen's apartment indulges all her needs and whims.

Kirsty, a hard-working model, fills long hours with a hectic schedule and travels all over the globe, often when she'd rather be at home surrounded by comfort and serenity. For her, home has to be a sanctuary from the outside world. Kirsty herself was the inspiration for our beautification plans: An angel both in temperament and appearance, she belongs in an aerie in the clouds. When the pressures of earthly life deplete her spirits, she can fly away home to her secret haven.

Kirsty

How at Heaven's gate
she claps her wings'
The morn not waking
till she sings

—JOHN LYLY

Foyer We decided to imbue the portal to Kirsty's heavenly hideaway with the spirit of a mischievous nymph. Whenever she arrives home, she will instantly be cheered by the glitz of her entryway. Across the sliding doors of her coat closet we painted a string of shimmering silver stars that glitter like flashbulbs. The wall opposite the

front door also received a dose of silver paint, reflecting Kirsty's infatuation with Andy Warhol and All-American Pop. Everything on the wall—the wall itself, the shelf, the frame around the mirror—became silver, melting into a large, luminous sculpture.

We accentuated the room's mod atmosphere with purple highlights. A racy, two-inch-wide stripe of royal purple frames the entire space, and a purple feather boa drapes the mirror, an essential part of any foyer. To complement the mirror, we brought in a tiny velvet loveseat where Kirsty can pull off wet shoes or dirty boots the moment she steps inside. Candles and pictures of her friends add warmth to the space and welcome her home. All in all, a dazzling antechamber for an angel's abode.

Understanding Color

*M*ore than any other decorative element, color rules a room. It creates a mood and defines the space. Lighter colors open up a room, darker colors can make even a large space seem intimate. Different rooms call for different color schemes, each depending on your preferences. Here are some of my favorites:

- *Boudoirs and bedrooms: Blues, aquas, celadon, silver, and pinks provide a sensuous backdrop for playing, relaxing, and eating. Richer tones such as pumpkin and burgundy impart an aura of romance when lit by candlelight and accessorized with tapestries and giant throws.*

- *Living rooms and salons: Chamois cream, pale yellows, emerald, and reds are ideal for entertaining, stimulating the mind and enlivening conversation.*

- *Dressing rooms: Navy and silver harmonize with mirrors to create a clean and sleek atmosphere for beautifying the body. In a space dedicated solely to luxury, enjoy the flexibility of using any colors you like; contrasting combinations of lights and darks work especially well.*

Bedroom   We wanted to transform Kirsty's bedroom into a paradise on earth where she can spoil herself as well as get her much-needed rest. Our first challenge  was space—not that the room is small, but it houses a six-foot-tall sylph under eight-foot-high ceilings. To give the room a sense of infinite expanse, we had Janusz and Kaori, our muralists, turn the ceiling into a slice of the heavens. They started with the shade of blue the sky takes on in the day's most magical hours and added fluffy cumulus clouds and endearing little angels. Extending the mural down the upper part of the walls, they magnified the illusion of depth. Now Kirsty has plenty of room to stretch her wings.

The muralists sustained the blissful theme on the bedroom's three white doors, covering them with trompe l'oeil paintings of ancient ruins. Our heads filled with images of dreamy walks among the gods of Olympus or Valhalla. Unfortunately, the ungainly steam radiator snapped our mood back down to earth; we solved that problem by finishing it in a suitably rapturous oil-based gold paint. We then prepared the two windows by simply adding curtain rods. Using white velvet and a diaphanous blue fabric, we made curtains by clipping the blue over the white with pronged café hooks; we contrived billows and gathers as we went. We then hung the curtains and used more of the sparkling blue fabric to create swags at the top of each window and one in between. A little stuffing helped pouf out the swags to match the clouds on the ceiling.

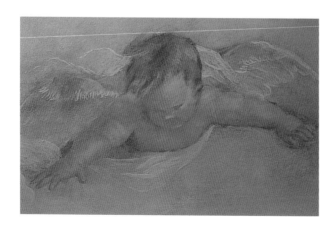

Flowered sheets, plenty of pillows, and a thick down comforter covered in velvet and satin turned Kirsty's bed into her own private cloud. Above, we devised a simple chiffon canopy to shelter our cherub while she sleeps. Screwing a hook into the ceiling, we hung the chiffon on a large ring that allows the fabric to slide freely for the desired look. Nails didn't work on the ceiling, so we used pieces of self-stick Velcro to hold the canopy's sides when

we swept them back into wings. Whenever she likes, Kirsty can let the sides down into a flowing, fluttering veil.

The only additional furniture we brought into the bedroom were some night tables where Kirsty can store books and journals. She already had a lackluster chest of drawers that she'd bought in desperation at a store that sells unfinished furniture. The right paint job soon turned it into a more celestial dresser. After applying a white base coat to seal the wood, we framed the drawers with tape and added a quick, framed rinceau in pink and gold to the fronts of the drawers. When we found antique French drawer pulls at a flea market, we replaced the dresser's original plain knobs. This finished our work; now Kirsty can soar far from the stresses of her busy life and repose in her own little corner of the sky.

*J*anice owns a shop called Candlelande where she sells the candles and candle-

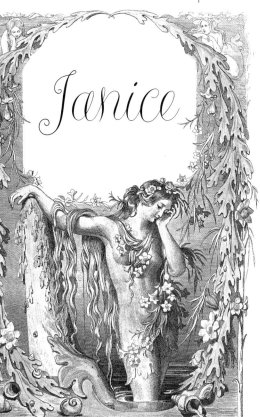

Janice

holders she crafts of wax and wrought iron. The shop and its wares have a distinctly gothic flavor, as does the image Janice herself projects to the world. Her inner self, however, prefers oceans to castles. Deeply spiritual, she feels a kinship with the creatures of the deep and dreams of swimming with dolphins. She asked us to help her convert her cramped city walk-up into a sublime lair for a sea goddess.

*Since once I sat upon
a promontory,
And heard a mermaid
on a dolphin's back
Uttering such dulcet
and harmonious breath,
That the rude sea
grew civil at her song,
And certain stars shot
madly from their spheres
To hear the sea-maid's music.*

—WILLIAM SHAKESPEARE

Bedroom Before we arrived on the scene, Janice had painted her 8 × 10 foot bedroom silver and turquoise. Although far more appealing than the typical white box many New Yorkers live in, the room still felt too close for comfort. We asked our muralists, Janusz and Kaori, to turn the space into a fanciful underwater theater where Janice's fantasies would be free to flow with the tide. Using rich blues and greens, they evoked undulating deep-sea currents that give the room a greater sense of depth.

Inspired by memories of crashing waves at the beach, we summoned the essence of whitecaps with a canopy on one side of the room. We bought several yards of inexpensive white cotton/rayon poet's shirt fabric, but found that we could not hammer nails into the tin ceiling. Instead, we made use of a preexisting hook above the bed. Asymmetrical swags tacked to

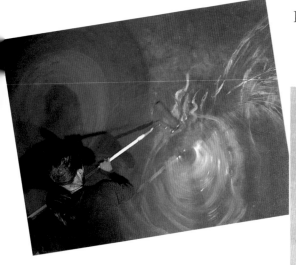

Shades and Nuances

—

Using a few shades of the same color can add depth and sophistication to your decorating scheme. You can either choose a few shades from the same swatch and have them pre-mixed, or you can buy the darkest of your desired hues and lighten it with varying amounts of flat or semigloss white.

the wall at one end converged on this central hook; the result elicits the sensation of standing at the bottom of the ocean and looking up at the rippling surface.

Across the room, on the wall by the dressing area, we constructed lush swags of silver stretch satin and blue stretch velvet. Here we drilled several hooks into the ceiling and wrapped them in silk organza to suggest Poseidon's trident. Trailing the satin and velvet from one hook to another, we let it stream to the floor and collect in swirling pools. Depending on her mood, Janice can leave the drapery down for drama or tie it back for simplicity.

We dressed the bed to resemble the gleaming interior of a giant clamshell, where a sea goddess might curl up to sleep. Moving her original bedspread from the top of the bed to between the mattress and box spring, we fashioned a

swaying dust ruffle. Atop the mattress we laid an extravagant featherbed, covering it with a giant satin curtain to create an alluring reef where any passing Neptune might be tempted to pause for a while. Settled on this shimmering nest, Janice can keep warm beneath a vintage 1940s satin comforter that we added. A jumble of pillows—some covered in fresh white cotton and others in cream satin trimmed with blue—offers a sumptuous place for our aquatic queen to rest her regal head.

For her dressing area, Janice found a severely distressed vanity at a flea market and worked miracles on it. Filling in the cracks and peeling veneer with wood putty, she finished it with aluminum paint and added navy blue highlights. The

restored piece makes not only a magnificent vanity, but a convenient storage space. We noticed how its mirrors made her room seem larger, so we decided to expand on the idea. The flea market yielded a mirrored night table and lingerie chest; we simply replaced the cracked mirrors and found the right place for them. Since Janice prefers candles to electric lights, lighting played only a minor part in our improvements. We simply added a pair of matching table lamps with shades that we dyed blue, and held back her canopy along the wall with candle sconces. Then we left Janice alone to drift off on her undersea reveries.

James & Irene

A truly talented hat designer, James has a keen sense of style and a passion for perfection. His taste in interiors tends toward the Victorian and Edwardian—ornate and intricate, but not stuffy. James lives with his best friend, Irene, a costume stylist for films, and has filled their apartment with turn-of-the-century taxidermy, ritual jewelry, and tribal costumes. Feeling a little out of step with modern times, he's an armchair explorer of sorts. His Stanley and Living-stone aura makes us think of Lake Victoria, the jungles of India, the Royal Geographical Society. The British empire's finest years would provide the inspiration for our refurbishing of James and Irene's living room and James's hat salon.

God is in the details
—ANONYMOUS

Living Room

The typical collector, James had carefully chosen pieces with a history. Many of his peculiar and beloved objects had become a part of his own history, but he had not figured out how to make the most of their visual appeal. He and Irene had simply scattered them about among Irene's furniture in a typical roommates' mishmash. All they needed was a fresh eye to see the potential of their space and of the pieces they already owned.

We started with the window, adding a valance and draperies to evoke the classic Victorian drawing

room. The valance, which we found at a flea market, had two panels attached to it and also came with two loose panels in the same fabric. We hung the valance over the window and tacked up one of the panels to the left of the window, making it look larger. In conjunction with the nearby bookshelf and the radiator, the second panel became an enclosed window seat secured with brads.

The rest of our work consisted of revamping and rearranging furniture, relocating knickknacks, and adding a few pieces. At a flea market, James found two mohair chairs, which Irene had reupholstered. We paired them with footstools that had previously held plants and now served as mini side tables. Another side table went next to the window seat. Although the sofa had already been recovered, Irene had been considering the addition of trim to hide its bare legs (how Victorian!). When James came home with some harmonious blue-and-olive lace, we instantly tacked it to the sofa's bottom edge. Artfully arranged

throws and pillows put the finishing touches on the furniture.

The room now had real form, but it needed some improvements in lighting. We added pleated silk shades trimmed with fringe to their chandelier. To supplement the one silk-shaded lamp they already had, we placed a lamp on the window seat's side table for twilight reading, and arrayed a few others around the room. All in all, a big improvement.

We brought new life to their many knickknacks by relocating them and finding new spots where they could be displayed. Pictures and mementoes created collages across the bookshelves, birds perched on teapot handles—the list goes on. In the end, James and Irene were astonished by the difference a simple rearrangement made in their living room. Like Queen Victoria and Prince Albert, they immediately sat down to high tea in the parlor.

> *Let each man have the*
> *wit to go his own way.*
> —Propertius

Salon James's salon, where he meets with his clients, required a very different approach. Here, starting with a large, empty, warehouse loft, we would create a dazzling Paris Apartment style showroom absolutely from scratch. After discussing the options, we started with the plaster and brick walls. We decided on a rinceau treatment and sat down with pencil and paper to design the moldings. Translating the drawings to real life, we used painter's tape to

lay out the walls and get a sense of how the moldings would actually look. Then we measured and located a

lumberyard where we could buy the molding for a great price. We'd have to cut it to size ourselves, but that would be easy. Ordering a bit more than we needed—just to be on the safe side—we sawed and glued and hammered. *Voilà!* James's salon now had the shell for his showroom.

Next we moved on to painting. James wanted a space that would act as a backrop without overshadowing his hats, so we started with a flat cream color. On top of that, we spread a wash made of a muddy, ruddy latex mixed with water. A sponge mop covered the broad surfaces, while a handheld sponge added some extra color at the corners of the rinceau. The walls aged before our eyes, taking on a worn, nicotine-stained look. To set off the rinceau, we added just a touch of gold.

The salon has two large, factory-style windows that called for simple and understated curtains. To keep costs down, James found yards and yards of inexpensive cotton muslin that hangs beautifully and lets natural light filter in. At the top of each window, we hung a mirrored valance, then hung the curtains simply by

tacking them to the wood backing with pushpins. If James decides later that he wants more substantial drapery, he can use the muslin underneath for sheers. Muslin also forms a curtain that divides James's work space from the showroom.

Meeting early in the morning over a month of Saturdays and Sundays, we accompanied James to flea markets and auctions to find furniture. Many of the pieces he bought had been overlooked by previous shoppers because they featured an awful hue of wood, had been badly painted, or were blighted with ugly upholstery. None of these superficial flaws bothered James; he bought them for their interesting shapes and solid workmanship. The oval conference table, for instance, had two extra legs that

Rinceau Riches

Transform a plain, ordinary wall into an architectural wonder with a rinceau treatment. With a little paint and ingenuity, you can make these decorative moldings look like they've always been there, imparting an air of history to any room. If you already have some rinceau, continue the theme with added rinceau on other walls and in other rooms.

1   Look in architectural books and magazines for design ideas and sample layouts. Give your wall its basic coat of paint.

2   Measuring carefully, lay out your plan on your wall.

3   Buy the molding of your choice at a lumberyard, always getting a little extra in case of mistakes.

4   Using a hand saw and a miter box (for 45° angles), cut the molding into segments corresponding to your rinceau dimensions.

5   Attach the molding to the wall with hot glue and finishing nails. Fill in nail holes and gaps with caulking.

6   If desired, add ornaments and details (available at the lumberyard) at the corners and in the center.

7   Before you put it up, paint the trim to match or contrast with the wall, enhancing dimension and substance with darker shades at the corners.

CYNTHIA ROWLEY

BETH HUTCHENS
ASSISTANT PRODUCTION MANAGER

looked awkward, but we discovered that they could easily be unscrewed. The reverse was true for a showcase that James already had: It just didn't look right until he found some large carved legs for it.

James happily took on the task of restoring each and every piece, which included a vanity-turned-desk, several chairs, and a number of nightstands-turned-side tables. His refinishing technique went as follows: After roughing up the piece with sandpaper, he primed it and applied the first coat of paint, usually a cream or pale green. He then added any gold highlights he wanted and gave the whole piece a coat of quick-drying, water-based polyurethane. A tawny blend of dark shades—olive, burnt sienna and rusty orange—mixed with a bit of water went on next. He brushed it on evenly, letting it drip naturally and fill in crevices. Sponging off the excess, he let it dry and added highlights in the original base color. The overall effect is one of subtle, genteel age.

James also reupholstered the seats and arm pads of the chairs, which had been covered with a nasty 1960s stripe. It was simple to remove the original fabric and trace the patterns onto heavy paper. The patterns guided James as he cut the new fabric;

he then fastened it to the seats and arm pads with upholstery tacks and glue. Complete at last, the furniture made itself right at home in the salon.

We secured a gigantic mirror to one wall with **L** brackets and then turned our attention to lighting. The focal point, a flea market chandelier, was truly a diamond in the rough when we found it. Hanging it from a

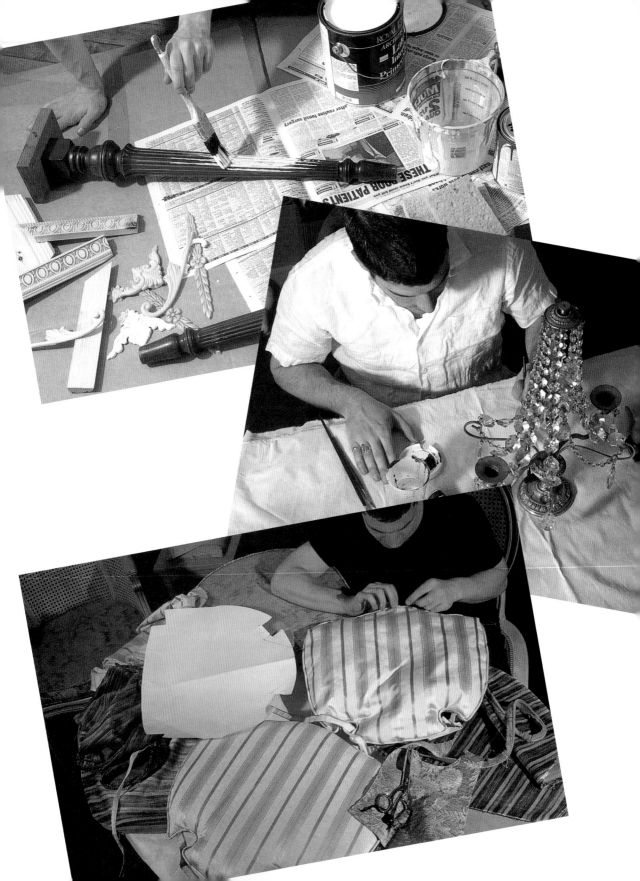

garment rack, we used needle-nosed pliers to remove the dingy dangling crystals. We soaked them for five minutes in a mixture of soapy water and bleach, donning rubber gloves and stirring gently. When we removed them from the bath, we wiped them clean and reattached them to the chandelier with the pliers. We replaced several missing crystals with new ones, then James trimmed the six shades with a rim of green velvet. Finally, we hung the glittering teardrop in the center of the salon.

We found two standing chandeliers to place on either side of the great mirror. They needed some easy rewiring, and James decided he didn't like their brassy gold finish. He bronzed them with a dark latex mixture that he devised, and covered their candleholders with velvet and scraps of the chair upholstery.

James's hats and a few fresh flowers were all the decoration the salon required. We fashioned a floral centerpiece for the conference table and placed it on a bed of feathers. With his hats on display, James had what he wanted: a fantasy salon in the heart of New York's garment district. Somehow, it seemed a thousand miles away, in a courtier's showroom off the continent; another place and time.

Furniture Refinishing Made Easy

To spruce up a piece of wood furniture that has not been painted, follow these simple steps:

1. *Rub it down with fine steel wool or a palm sander to prepare the surface.*

2. *Apply the stain of your choice with a cotton cloth (this helps prevent drips).*

3. *When dry, buff the surface with a clean cloth.*

4. *Clean inside drawers and cabinets using steel wool and butcher's wax.*

s seen in

MANHATTAN FI[...]

AS SEEN IN

VOGU[E]

THE IMPORTA[...]
a [...]

Sources

If we go down into
ourselves we find that
we possess exactly what
we desire.

—SIMONE WEIL

Indulge your endless instincts …

$\mathcal{I}$f finding the inspiration to redo your apartment is the heart of the Paris Apartment idea, knowing how to shop for furnishings is the mind. Most Americans are experts at spending money, but few take the time to find the value in timeworn things. Knowing how to *see*, the key to inspiration, is also the key to finding the perfect old ottoman or reading lamp.

Before I opened my shop, I spent every Saturday afternoon at the flea market, not necessarily looking for anything in particular. Sometimes I'd be overwhelmed by the wealth of beautiful things at my fingertips. Still, I didn't quite understand my obsession until the day I spotted a wonderful hand-painted French vanity. Its deeply carved details were coated with cracked and dirty paint, but it inspired me to begin creating my boudoir. Once I got started, my instincts led me to the next piece, and the next . . .

It was during this process that I learned the cardinal rule of shopping at flea markets and auctions: Get there early. You won't be alone if you arrive at dawn. And don't be intimidated by auctions. Although they have a highbrow reputation, they are, in fact, attended by people just like you and me. There are many types of auctions, including some that require you to call in advance for tickets. Even the high-end auctions have items of interest for price-conscious buyers, though you should set a definite spending limit before you go. Allow yourself enough time before the bidding starts to peruse the offerings and note which items interest you. Then bid whatever you like within your limits, and don't feel con-

Finding Sources

Where can you find the incredible vintage fabrics and furnishings that will make your home a Paris Apartment? Architecture and design magazines are filled with advertising and pointers, as are trade periodicals and collectors' newsletters. Locally, newspapers and pennysavers can guide you to garage sales, antiques shops, and flea markets; globally, the Internet contains an ever evolving number of Web sites, bulletin boards, and chat rooms where your questions can be answered.

strained by the increments set by the auctioneer. Bid with restraint, though, both in terms of numbers and demeanor. If you show too much excitement about an item, you're likely to spark someone else's enthusiasm and raise the stakes. Auctions can be great fun, but bear in mind that once you place a winning bid, you are required to pay for it; you can't back out after the heat of battle dies down.

*T*o find the truly great hidden treasures, learn to really look at a piece and study its details. First and foremost, look for craftsmanship and quality. These are the hallmarks of vintage pieces—after all, a piece that's lasted fifty years must be made pretty well. On the other hand, never assume that a piece in bad condition is unworthy. Many flaws can easily be fixed. Wobbly legs can be tightened, peeling veneer can be glued down, and torn upholstery can be replaced. If you're willing to sharpen your eye and spend some time on a piece, you'll be able to fill your home with gorgeous old furnishings for relatively little cash.

As you roam the flea markets and auctions, give yourself permission to mix and match styles and periods. Forcing yourself into a narrow design slot goes against every Paris Apartment philosophy. . . . You should have fun, let go, see

How to Shop

A rose among thorns.

—AMMIANUS MARCELLINAS

Flea Market Savvy

To find the real flea market bargains, you must be willing to dig deep. Go to the "lesser" markets and vendors that others often overlook. Bargains are everywhere! It may take a little more effort, but shopping is fun, after all. Just keep this mental checklist handy:

- *To save money and find hidden treasures, look for potential. Pay extra attention to items with cosmetic flaws that can be taken care of with a refinishing, reupholstering, or rewiring job. Although easily restored, these pieces are overlooked by most shoppers and underpriced by many vendors.*

- *Check for breaks. Structural problems such as broken arms or legs generally require the help of a professional. Broken pieces should be dirt cheap to be worth your while.*

- *Look for deep carving, a characteristic of genuine antiques.*

- *Check under peeling paint to see the original finish, which may well be worth restoring.*

- *Peek under the upholstery to examine the original fabric. No longer manufactured today, many old fabrics have a rare and special charm.*

- *Don't be put off by rusty metal. Hinges, knobs, and pulls can be replaced, while metal furniture can be spray-painted.*

where your fantasies take you! Mix a baroque table with Louis XIV chairs; they'll go together simply because they're beautiful. If you want to establish a link between varied pieces, paint them along similar lines or use complementary fabrics to reupholster. You can choose fabrics themselves, as well as knick-knacks, tableware, and other details according to the same principles. Trust

your sense of color; forget the rules of conventional decorating and focus on what appeals to *you*. If you love each and every piece, you can make them work together.

You can find all sorts of one-of-a-kind objects at flea markets and auctions. Even pieces that were mass-produced in the 1930s and 1940s are rare collectors' items today. If you know what to look for, it's not all that difficult to determine when an item was made. Check under layers of fabric to determine if the piece has been reupholstered. Fabric from the 1960s or 1970s may conceal a much older layer of velvet or damask. The same goes for layers of paint. I can't count the number of times I've stripped furniture for refinishing only to discover a beautiful mural or hand-painted design concealed below. Look closely to see what others may have missed—it's a real thrill to uncover hidden prizes.

Another way to determine the age of a piece is to look for dovetailing at the joints of drawers. The meshing of two slotted edges indicates the kind of fine workmanship that many furniture makers have abandoned in favor of nails and staples. Examine hinges, knobs, and locks; modern hardware often has telltale seams or shallow stamped designs instead of deep carving. Check inside drawers for labels that may reveal when a piece was made. European lettering or numbers on a piece may indicate that it was brought over from the "old country" by somebody's great-grandfather. Turn a chest of drawers around to detect signs of weathering on the back. Are there termite holes from years gone by? Likewise, signs of wear and tear on frequently used parts indicate the passage of time.

When appraising the value of a piece, estimate how much you will have to spend to bring it back to life. Will you need to hire a professional to recane that seat? Can you touch up chipped paint yourself? New upholstery can do wonders for a vintage piece. Almost anyone can handle the basics, but you'll need to find a professional to take care of more complex problems. The art of tufting, for instance, has all but

been lost. When you come across shaky arms and legs, find out if a screw is loose or if the piece is actually broken. Broken joint dowels can be replaced and reglued, or they can be removed and the joint can be secured with wood glue alone.

Anything goes in the Paris Apartment, as long as it has real beauty and speaks to your soul. So start shopping. . . . And have fun!

Restoring a Chandelier

You've found a graceful old chandelier at the flea market and brought it home, but it doesn't sparkle like it could. What to do? A cleaning and a few easy repairs can bring it back to life.

1   Mix a bucket of warm, soapy water with a bit of bleach. Using needle-nose pliers, remove one strand of crystals at a time, and immerse. Soak for 10 to 15 minutes, swirling gently with your hands. Rinse and lay on paper towels to dry. Replace the strand and repeat the process with the next one.

2   When all the crystal strands are finished, remove and clean any individual crystals in the same manner, using a toothbrush on any hard-to-reach spots.

3   Replace missing or broken crystals with spares bought new or at the flea market. Attach them with wire cut with pliers.

4   Add extra crystals or glass beads, baubles, fruits, or drops to enliven and customize your chandelier.

5   Add tiny shades dyed and trimmed to match your decor.

Resources

Auctions

Dutch Auction
Mickleton, NJ
609–423–6800

One of the largest auctions in the nation. Very informal with an incredible variety of antiques, used furniture, rugs, chandeliers, and more.

S&S Auction
Repaupo, NJ
800–343–4979

Similar to Dutch, with lots of buried treasures in its three-acre outside lot.

South Jersey Auction
Repaupo, NJ
609–467–4834

Smallest of the three, still filled with lots of eclectic merchandise.

Lubin Galleries Auction House
Chelsea Antiques Building, 10th Floor
110 East 25th Street
New York, NY
212–929–0909

Auctions on Thursday evenings. Open Monday through Friday for previewing and placing bids.

Tepper Galleries
110 East 25th Street
New York, NY
212–677–5300

Manhattan auction, some bargains, lots of interesting pieces, a little more structured than the country auctions.

Flea Markets

26th Street and 6th Avenue
New York, NY
212–243–5343

New York's largest flea market.

The Garage
25th Street, between 6th and 7th Avenues
New York, NY

Two floors of a parking garage transform into a market year round on the weekends.

The Annex
6th Avenue and 27th Street
New York, NY

Vendors have a wide variety of merchandise, and some of the best bargains.

The Grand Bazaar
25th Street, between 6th Avenue and Broadway
New York, NY

Outdoor market held year round, every weekend.

SOHO Antiques and Flea Market
Corner of Grand Street and Broadway
New York, NY
212–682–2000

Flea market of the Lower East Side.

PS 44
76th Street and Columbus Avenue
New York, NY
212–974–6302

Combinaton of old and new merchandise. Bargains vary.

Lambertville Antique Market
Route 29
Lambertville, NJ
609–397–0456

Outdoor flea market, all used merchandise, some authentic antiques, and lots of used furniture and accessories.

Englishtown Auction Sales
90 Wilson Avenue
Englishtown, NJ
908–446–9644

Very large flea market; indoor and outdoor merchandise.

Route 70 Flea Market
117 Route 70
Lakewood, NJ

Indoor and outdoor flea market; hundreds of vendors.

Saturday's Flea Market
3751 East Harrisburg Pike
Middletown, PA

True "flea market," with hundreds of dealers.

Quaker City Flea Market, Inc.
Tacony and Comly Streets
Philadelphia, PA
215–744–2022

Called the oldest flea market in Philadelphia.

Woodbury Antiques and Flea Market
Route 6
Woodbury, CT
203–263–2841

One of the oldest markets in Connecticut.

Special Shows

Antique Garage Sale
175 Route 303
Valley Cottage, NY
914–268–1730

This group travels and shops in order to hold a sale on the first Sunday of every month. Great prices and varied merchandise.

Atlantique City
Atlantic City Convention Center
Atlantic City, NJ
800–526–2724

Biannual show (October and March), filled with antiques and collectibles, with hundreds of dealers.

Brimfield Show
Brimfield, MA
413–245–9556

The town of Brimfield hosts a gigantic flea market in May, July, and September each year.

Great American Antiquefest
Phoenix, NY
315–695–6115

520 dealers gather at this annual sale with a huge variety of wares.

Madison Bouckville
Route 20
Bouckville, NY
315–824–2462

Annual outdoor show with 1,000 dealers, and lots of varied merchandise.

Shops

Antiques on Houston
Houston and Elizabeth Streets
New York, NY

Indoor and outdoor (weather permiting) store with everything including statues, fixtures, used furniture, and lighting.

Antique Salon
870 Lexington Avenue
New York, NY
212–472–3358

This upscale salon is chock full of painted furniture, chandeliers, and boudoir accessories.

Antiques USA
Kennebunk-Arundel, ME
207–985–7766

Huge store with low prices.

Archangel Antiques
334 East 9th Street
New York, NY
212–260–9313

Eclectic mix of furniture, knick-knacks, vanity and dresser antiques.

Candlelande
305 East 9th Street
New York, NY
212–260–8386

Gothic castle full of handmade candles and wrought-iron candelabras, sconces, and accessories needed to create the perfect fifteenth-century chamber.

Chelsea Antiques Building
110 West 25th Street
New York, NY
212–929–0909

Twelve floors of books, antiques, linens, furniture, and collectibles.

Cobblestones
314 East 9th Street
New York, NY
212–673–5372

Some furniture, but mostly a terrific mix of almost every style.

The Front Porch
309 Main Street
Port Washington, NY
516–944–6868

Family-run shop with a vast selection of used furniture and antiques.

Gotham Galleries
80 Fourth Avenue at 10th Street
New York, NY
212–677–3303

Two floors of used furniture, lights, tapestries, and antiques.

Housing Works Thrift Shops
143 West 17th Street
202 East 77th Street
New York, NY
212–772–8461

Irreplaceable Artifacts
14 Second Avenue and Houston Street
New York, NY
212–505–0700

High quality of merchandise and fascinating variety.

Live Shop Die
151 Avenue A
New York, NY
212–674–7265

Variety of goods.

Lucille's
127 West 26th Street
New York, NY

Often you have to dig, but there is always something special to uncover.

Nadine's
East 7th Street, between First and
Second Avenues
New York, NY

Linens and antiques from the twenties, thirties, and forties.

A Repeat Performance
156 First Avenue
New York, NY
212–529–0832

Used goods including furniture and
accessories with lots of style.

Ritz Thrift Shop
107 West 57th Street
New York, NY
212–265–4559

Second Chance Antiques
10th and Walnut Streets
Philadelphia, PA
215–627–4416

Used furniture and miscellaneous
hodgepodge.

Tell Five Friends
East 5th Street, between First and
Second Avenues
New York, NY

Completely full of used and one-of-
a-kind items.

Shops in Paris

Besson
32 rue Bonaparte
Phone: 40 51 89 64

Excellent source for authentic wall-
papers in a variety of patterns.

Capeline
144 avenue de Versailles
Phone: 45 20 22 65

New and reproductions of old
lampshades.

Fanette
1 rue d'Alencon
Phone: 42 22 21 73

Wonderful source for vintage
French linens.

La Passsementerie Nouvelle
15 rue Etienne Marcel
Phone: 42 36 30 01

In-house reproduction of luxurious
trims from French castles. They also
reproduce original furniture pieces
with superior craftsmanship.

Antique Buying Trips

Through the Looking Glass
Charlotte, NC
704–333–2109

Shopping trips to England and
France, including airfare, hotel, and
introductions to sources and trade
warehouses for real antiques.

Publications

Garage Sale & Flea Market Annual,
3rd Edition
Collector Books
PO Box 3009
Paducah, KY

$24.95. Resource of massive listings
nationwide.

Hudson Valley Antiquer
PO Box 561
Rhinebeck, NY

Free paper, or $18.95 yearly sub-
scription. Listings of shows, markets,
and sales.

Mass Bay Antiques
Ipswich, MA
508–777–7070

$15 per year subscription. News-
paper listing auctions, antique shows,
flea markets, estate sales, barn sales,
and group shows.

Suburban newspapers worldwide

Almost all newspapers have listings
for neighborhood estate sales, auctions, tag and garage sales, especially
in the summer. Look in the classified
section.

Treasure Chest Newspaper
Venture Publishing Company
New York, NY
212–496–2234

This can be picked up for free at
auctions and some antique shops, or
you can subscribe for about $25 per
year.

US Flea Market Directory
by Albert LaFarge
Avon Books
New York, NY

Extensive guide with maps and
directions covering the entire country.

Architectural Designs and Supplies

Dykes Lumber
348 West 44 Street
New York, NY
212–246–6480

Hardware and lumber store with a full range of trims and details for creating rinceau and ceiling treatments.

Raymond Enkeboll Designs
Carson, CA
310–532–1400

Architectural woodcarvings of all kinds.

Grand Brass and Lamps
221 Grand Street
New York, NY
212–226–2567

Candle covers for chandeliers, extra crystals, and anything you could possibly need to fix up that old lamp from the flea market.

Janovic Plaza
215 Seventh Avenue
New York, NY
212–645–5454

Variety of foam-core medallions for chandeliers, great for paints, stenciling kits, and curtain rods.

Just Bulbs
938 Broadway
New York, NY
212–228–7820

Full of all kinds of light: Christmas lights with stars, patio lights, and colored bulbs.

Pearl Paint
308 Canal Street
New York, NY
212–431–7932

Huge resource for canvas, custom paint, stained-glass paint, self-stick velcro. In-house hardware store.

SA Bendheim
122 Hudson Street
New York, NY
212–226–6370

Source for custom stained-glass materials, glass beads, and glass cutters.

Fabrics

Butterfly Fabrics
256 West 39th Street
New York, NY
212–575–5640

Stretch velvets, satins, and crinoline.

Lower East Side
Orchard Street
New York, NY

Best prices for lots of velvet and unusual fabrics from India or Morocco.

Harry Zarin
72 Grand and Allen Streets
New York, NY
212–966–0310

Great variety of satins, damasks, and muslin, especially remnant section.

M&J Trimmings
1008 Sixth Avenue
New York, NY
212–391–6200 or 391–9072

Abundant source for tassles, trims, and ribbon.

Muralists

Janusz Gilewicz & Kaori Kayo
Reflections of Light
271 East 10th Street, Suite 66
New York, NY 10009
Telephone & Fax: 212–475–7692

Janusz Gilewicz and Kaori Kayo of Reflections of Light are New York–based fine artists and muralists. Mr. Gilewicz, a political refugee from Kraków, came to New York in 1988 after spending three years painting movie sets in Rome. Ms. Kayo is a native of Okinawa, Japan, and came to New York in 1989. Both painters have had their work exhibited at numerous Manhattan art galleries, including Artopia, The Soho Gallery, and Artist's Space. The two formed Reflections of Light in 1994 and have executed mural commissions for stores, restaurants, and private homes throughout Manhattan. Their work has appeared in *Retail Shops in New York Interior and Display*, published by Noriaka Mizoguchi, and has been featured in national and international newspapers and magazines. Mr. Gilewicz's hand-painted leather jackets have been collected by such celebrities as Eric Clapton, Joe Cocker, Iggy Pop, Slash, Aaron Neville, and Kansai Yamamoto.

The Paris Apartment : Style Chart

Style	Historical Origin	Ambience
Greek Isles	900–200 BCE	aquatic, sunny, carefree
Roman Grotto	500 BCE–AD 300	cool, relaxed
Gothic	12th–16th centuries	mysterious, dark
Baroque/Rococo/ Neoclassical	17th–19th centuries	ornate, intimate, highly decorative
Victorian	late 19th century	formal, elegant, reserved
Art Nouveau	late 19th century	free-flowing, natural
Orient Express	early 20th century	worldly, sophisticated
Hollywood Golden Era	1920s–1940s	glamorous

Palette	Fabrics	Lighting	Low-Budget Finishing Touches
aqua, sea blues, pure whites	stripes, cotton	star shapes, glass shapes, sparkle	urns, potted palms, statuary, columns
greens	plentiful, flowing, terry cloth	sconces, candles, poolside mood	clay vases, fish tanks, pillows, ironwork
grays, gold, deep reds and blues	tapestry, velvet, damask	dim, candles, chandeliers, sconces	gargoyles, ironwork, church pieces
pinks, greens, pastels	silks, satins, velvets	chandeliers, standing chandeliers, candles	tassels for drawer pulls, fringed lampshades, french doors, mirrors
muted tones, burgundy, emerald	heavy velvets, damask	oil lamps, chandeliers, candles	red lampshades, lace draped over lampshades
many	light, floating	sleek, early modern, glass shades	triptych mirrors, mirrored furniture
red, gold, Moroccan	masculine, velvets, tassels	table lamps in pairs, luxurious lampshades, amber bulbs	leather boxes, old luggage, steamer trunks
pastels, silver	faux fur, animal prints, satins, silk	chandeliers, pairs of table lamps, candles	mirrors, sheepskins, flowers, bearskin rugs